Connie J. Schnoes, Ph.D.

Illustrated by Paige Schnoes-Anderson

Dedication

To my sons, Jordan & Colin, for being the first to tuck the Bedtime Pass under your pillows and keeping them there. To my husband, Dan, and our children, Whitney, Jordan, Morgan, Paige, Babbs (Abby) and Colin for your ongoing love, support and encouragement.

Acknowledgment

I would like to acknowledge Patrick Friman for saying "yes" all those years ago when I took up his offer to research the Bedtime Pass. Who knew it would lead to all that it has.

Moose Tracks Publishing
13518 L Street
Omaha, NE 68137
www.TheBedtimePass.com

ISBN: 978-0-9837110-2-5
Library of Congress Data on File with the Publisher.

Printed in the United States of America

10 9 8 7 6 5 4 3 2 1

THE BEDTIME PASS PARENT INSTRUCTIONS

The Bedtime Pass is recommended for children as young as three years old who delay (resist) falling asleep after bedtime and typically fall asleep in their beds alone. Follow these steps to use the Bedtime Pass procedure.

Step 1 Secure a Bedtime Pass. You can make one or order one from the **TheBedtimePass.com**. I recommend including your child in choosing their Bedtime Pass. He/she might not understand what it is and that is okay.

Step 2 Read this story, "The Bedtime Pass" to your child.

Step 3 Help your child place the Bedtime Pass under his/her pillow. Remind your child that he/she can come out or call out one time. And when he/she does he/she has to give you his/her Bedtime Pass.

Step 4 Tuck your child into bed as usual.

Step 5 When your child calls or comes out attend to him/her immediately. Meet the request if appropriate. Have your child give you his/her Bedtime Pass whether or not you met the specific request.

Step 6 Remind your child he/she has used his/her Bedtime Pass and so he/she cannot come out or call out again. Tell your child good night and leave.

Step 7 Do not respond to any further attempts to call out. If your child comes out of the bedroom at bedtime or during the night, simply return (guide) him/her back to bed (without speaking to him/her).

Step 8 In the morning praise your child for falling asleep quickly and staying in bed all night. Or praise him/her for falling asleep quickly and staying in bed all night after using the Bedtime Pass. Return the Bedtime Pass and have your child put it under his/her pillow.

Step 9 Repeat steps nightly.

Step 10 After several nights gradually decrease reminders about the Bedtime Pass. Simply prompt your child to make sure the Bedtime Pass is under his/her pillow.

*If sleep related struggles continue after you have tried the Bedtime Pass, ask your primary care provider for a referral to a behavioral pediatric sleep specialist in your community.

This is a story about
Jordan and Morgan,
two children who are
a lot like you.

They play outside.

They play at home.

They play at school.

Sometimes they play alone.

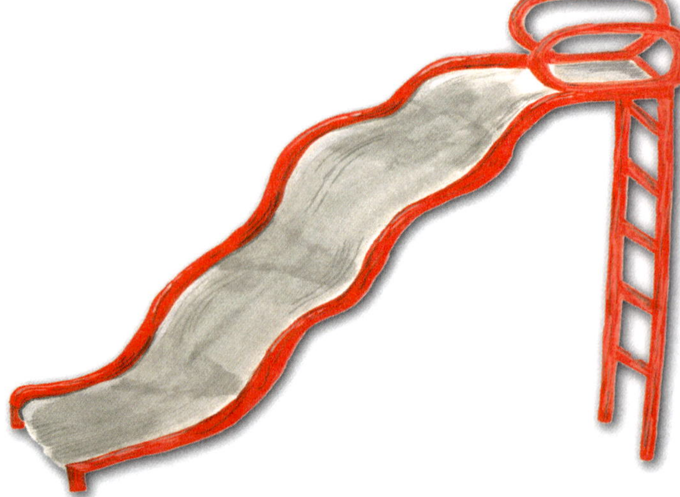

Sometimes they play together.

At the end of each busy day, it is time to get ready for bed.

Jordan and Morgan both love their evening snack.

Dad says "Jordan and Morgan!
It is 7:30. It is time to get ready for bed,
and it's bath night!"

After baths, they put on
their pajamas.

They brush their hair.

They brush their teeth.

They go potty.

And they
get drinks.

Finally, to their room they go...
for a storybook before bed.

Then it is time for hugs, prayers,
thank yous and I love yous.

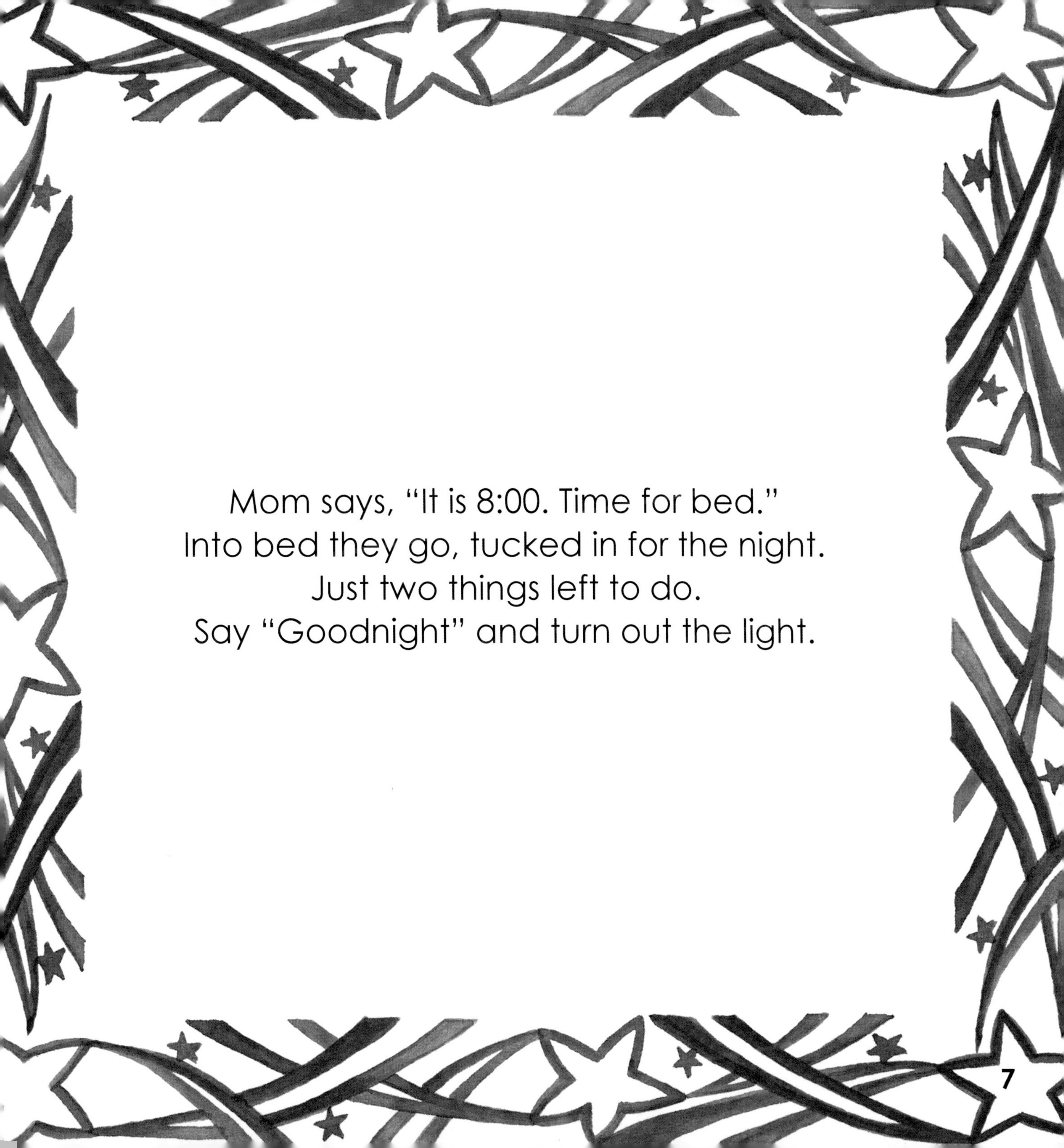

Mom says, “It is 8:00. Time for bed.”
Into bed they go, tucked in for the night.
Just two things left to do.
Say “Goodnight” and turn out the light.

"Goodnight
Morgan."

"Goodnight
Jordan."

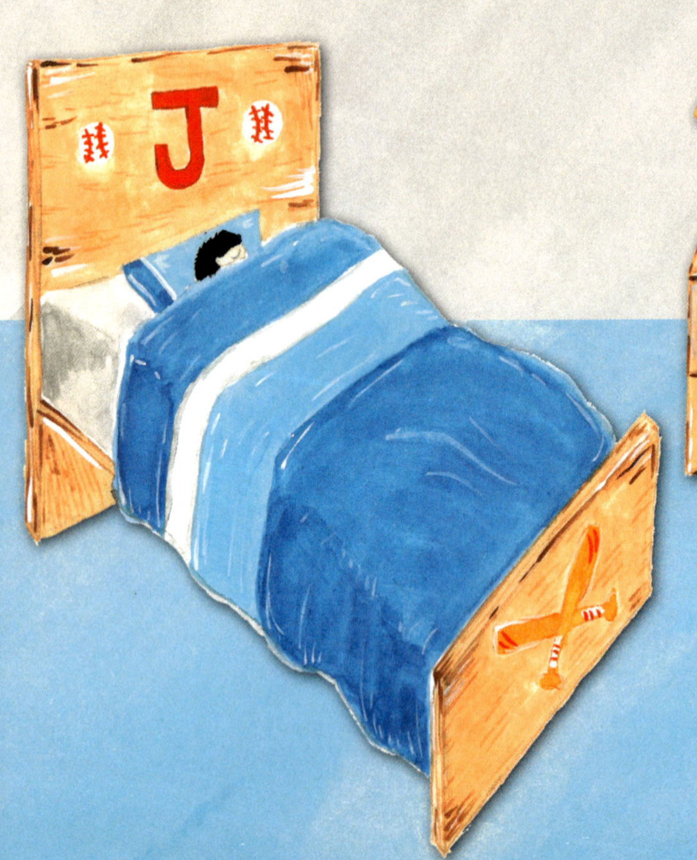

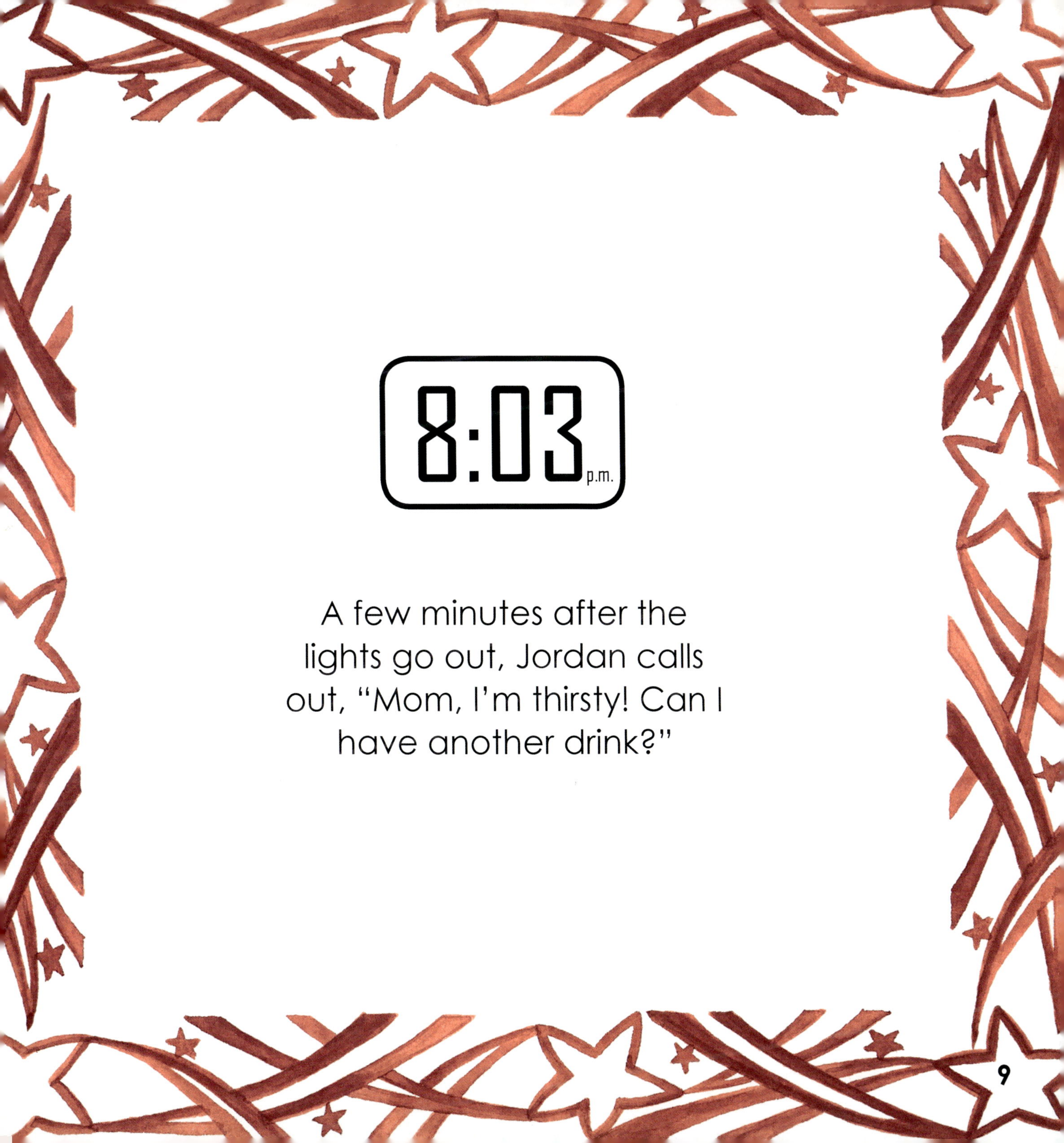

A few minutes after the lights go out, Jordan calls out, "Mom, I'm thirsty! Can I have another drink?"

Mom gets Jordan another drink and tucks him into bed again.

8:05 p.m.

"Goodnight Jordan, I love you. Now go to sleep."

8:14 p.m.

"Mom, We're scared. Will you turn on the hallway light?"

Mom turns on the hall light.

"Now children, go to sleep."

Just when all seems quiet, Morgan crawls out of bed and finds her Dad.

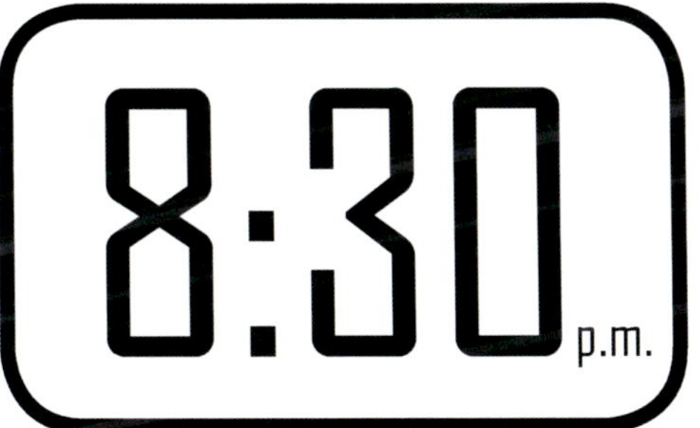

"Dad, can I have another hug?"

Dad hugs Morgan and takes her back to bed.

He goes back to his chair, and within minutes, Morgan is back again, this time asking for one more story.

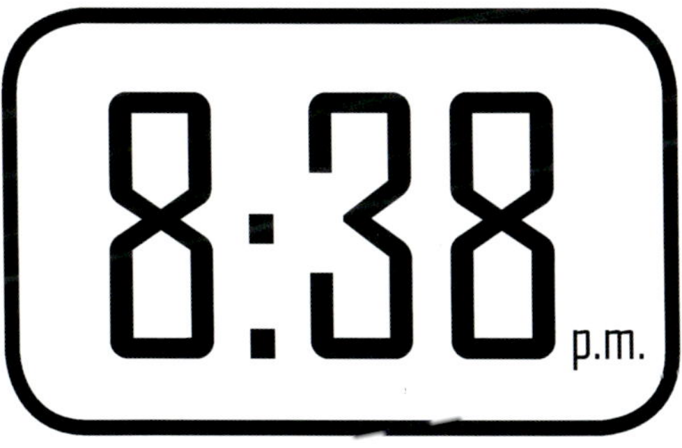

Dad says, "Morgan, it is time for bed. No more stories. Get back into bed."

Morgan starts to cry,
"Please, just one more story?"

8:40 p.m.

"Okay, Morgan. Just one more," says Mom. "Go pick out a book."

Jordan hears Mom reading a story and sneaks out to join them.

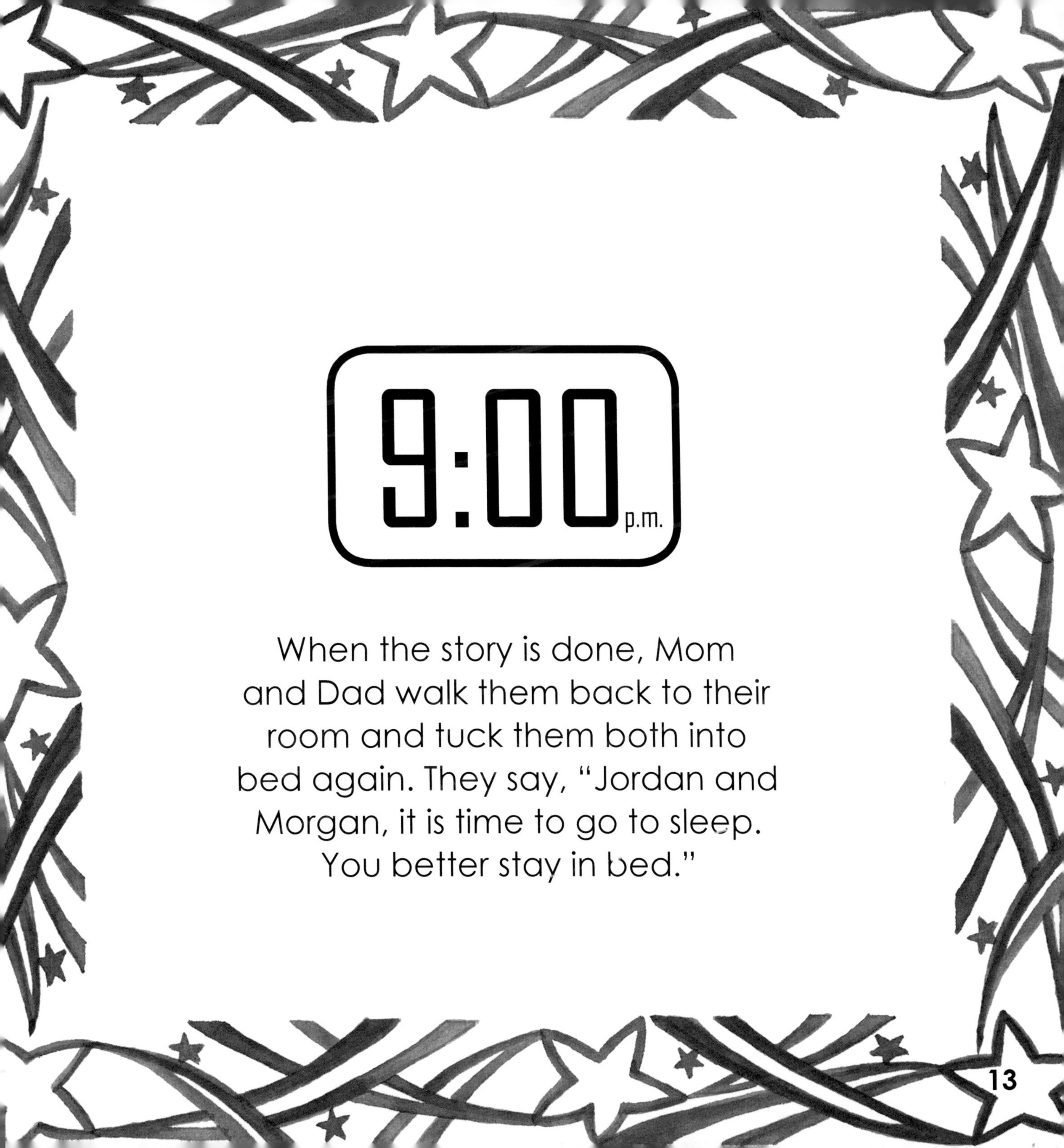

When the story is done, Mom and Dad walk them back to their room and tuck them both into bed again. They say, "Jordan and Morgan, it is time to go to sleep. You better stay in bed."

This happened night...

"Dad, can I have another hug?"

"Please Dad, just one more story?"

after night...

"Mom, I'm thirsty! Can I have another drink?"

"Mom, I'm scared. Will you turn on the hallway light?"

after night...

"Please Mom, just one more story?"

"Dad, I'm scared. Will you turn on the hallway light?"

after night...

"Dad, I'm thirsty! Can I have another drink?"

"Mom, can I have another hug?"

Mom and Dad look at each other, tired and frustrated, and Dad says, "We have to do something about bedtime. Jordan and Morgan need more sleep, and so do we."

The next day, Mom calls Dr. Connie and tells her all about their bedtime struggles. Dr. Connie says,

"It sounds like *The Bedtime Pass* is what you need.

It's a special pass that you give to each child.

They can use it only once per night if they get out of bed or they call out to you after they are in bed.

But it's important for them to give you the pass if they call out or come out."

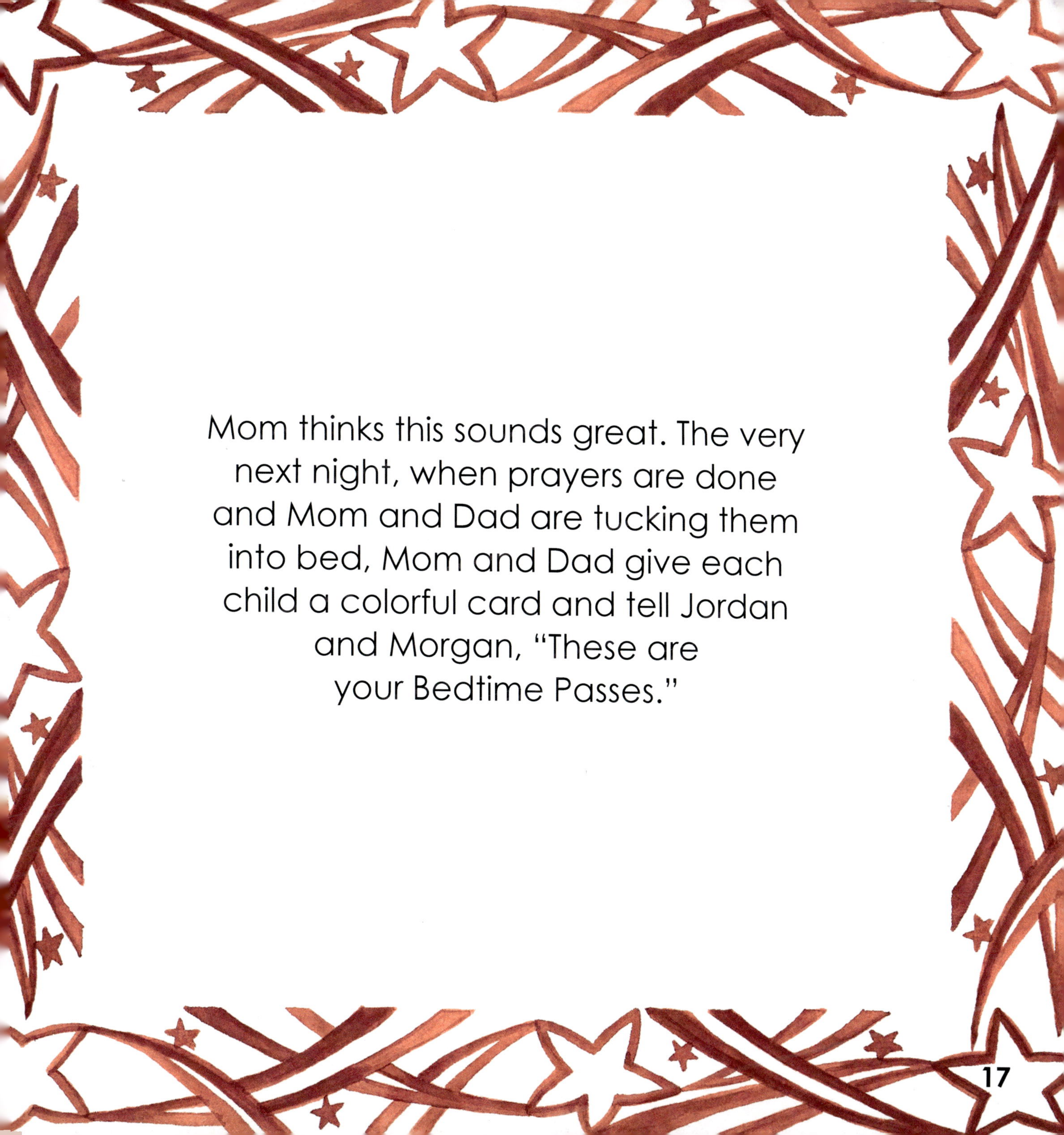

Mom thinks this sounds great. The very next night, when prayers are done and Mom and Dad are tucking them into bed, Mom and Dad give each child a colorful card and tell Jordan and Morgan, "These are your Bedtime Passes."

They explain, "*The Bedtime Pass* is good for one trip out of bed after lights are out or one time calling out for us to come back into the room."

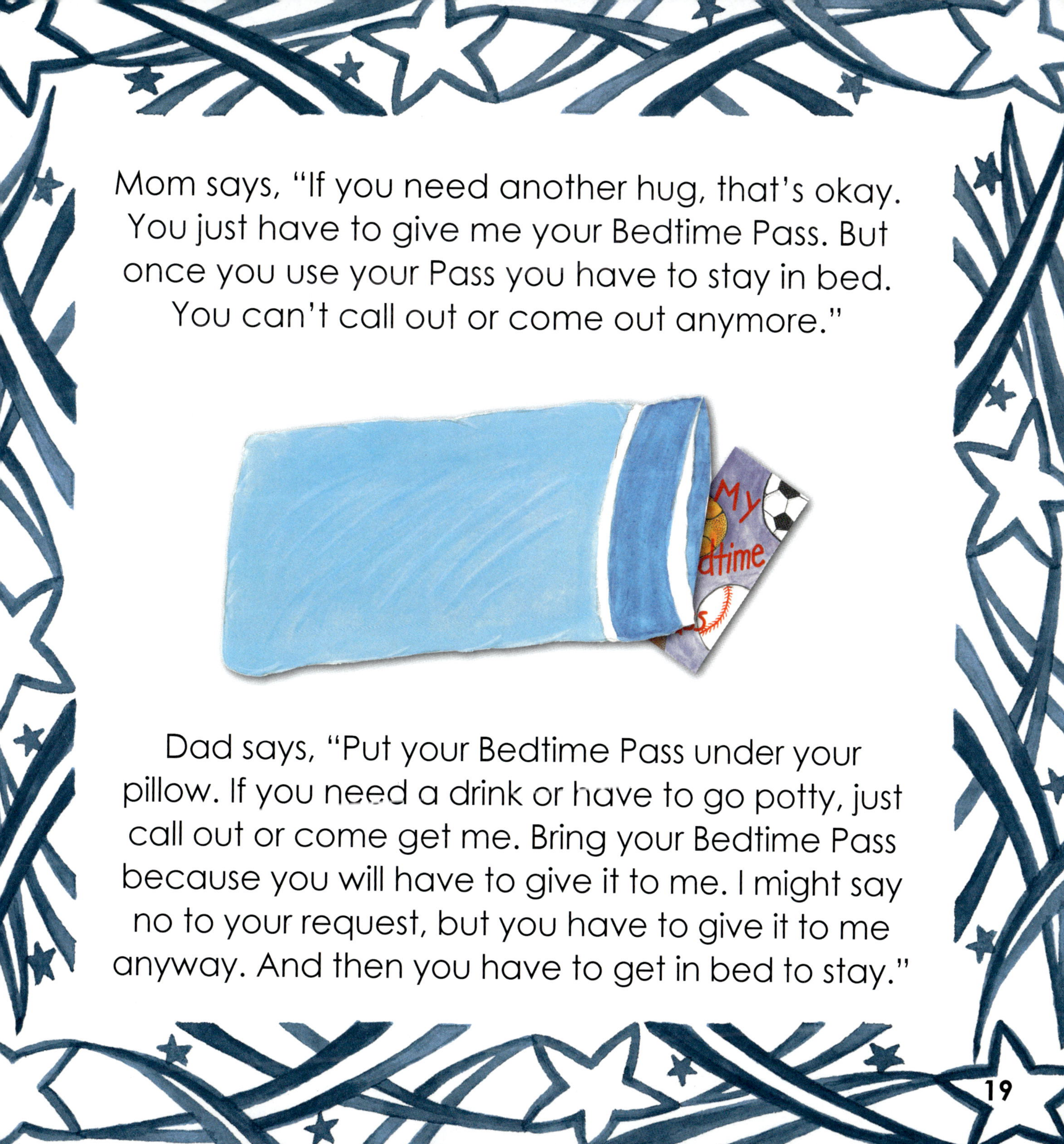

Mom says, "If you need another hug, that's okay. You just have to give me your Bedtime Pass. But once you use your Pass you have to stay in bed. You can't call out or come out anymore."

Dad says, "Put your Bedtime Pass under your pillow. If you need a drink or have to go potty, just call out or come get me. Bring your Bedtime Pass because you will have to give it to me. I might say no to your request, but you have to give it to me anyway. And then you have to get in bed to stay."

Jordan and Morgan are excited about their Bedtime Passes. They slide them under the pillows on their beds where they can keep them very handy.

Mom and Dad hug them goodnight and turn out the lights.

"Goodnight Jordan.
We love you."

"Goodnight Morgan.
We love you."

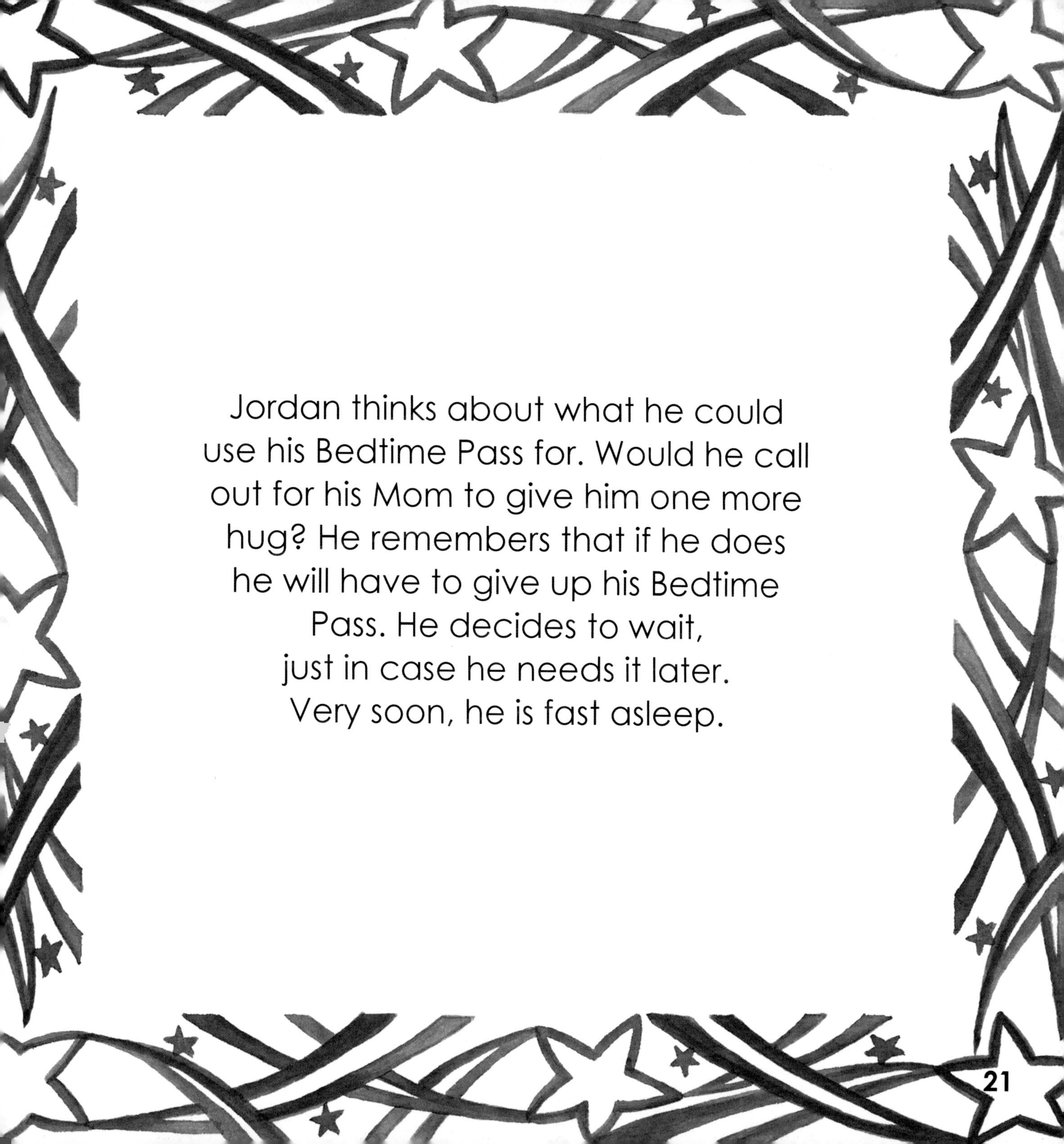

Jordan thinks about what he could use his Bedtime Pass for. Would he call out for his Mom to give him one more hug? He remembers that if he does he will have to give up his Bedtime Pass. He decides to wait, just in case he needs it later. Very soon, he is fast asleep.

Morgan thinks about her Bedtime Pass, too. But a few minutes after she is tucked into bed, Morgan gets out of bed and finds Mom and Dad. She asks for another bedtime story. Dad says, "Morgan, it is time for bed. No more stories."

Mom walks her back to bed and says, "Morgan, you have to give me your Bedtime Pass because you got out of bed."

Morgan slowly pulls her Bedtime Pass out from under her pillow and hands it to her Mom. She quietly climbs into bed. She feels sad about having to give up her Bedtime Pass. Now she can't get out of bed anymore. Morgan is in bed to stay.

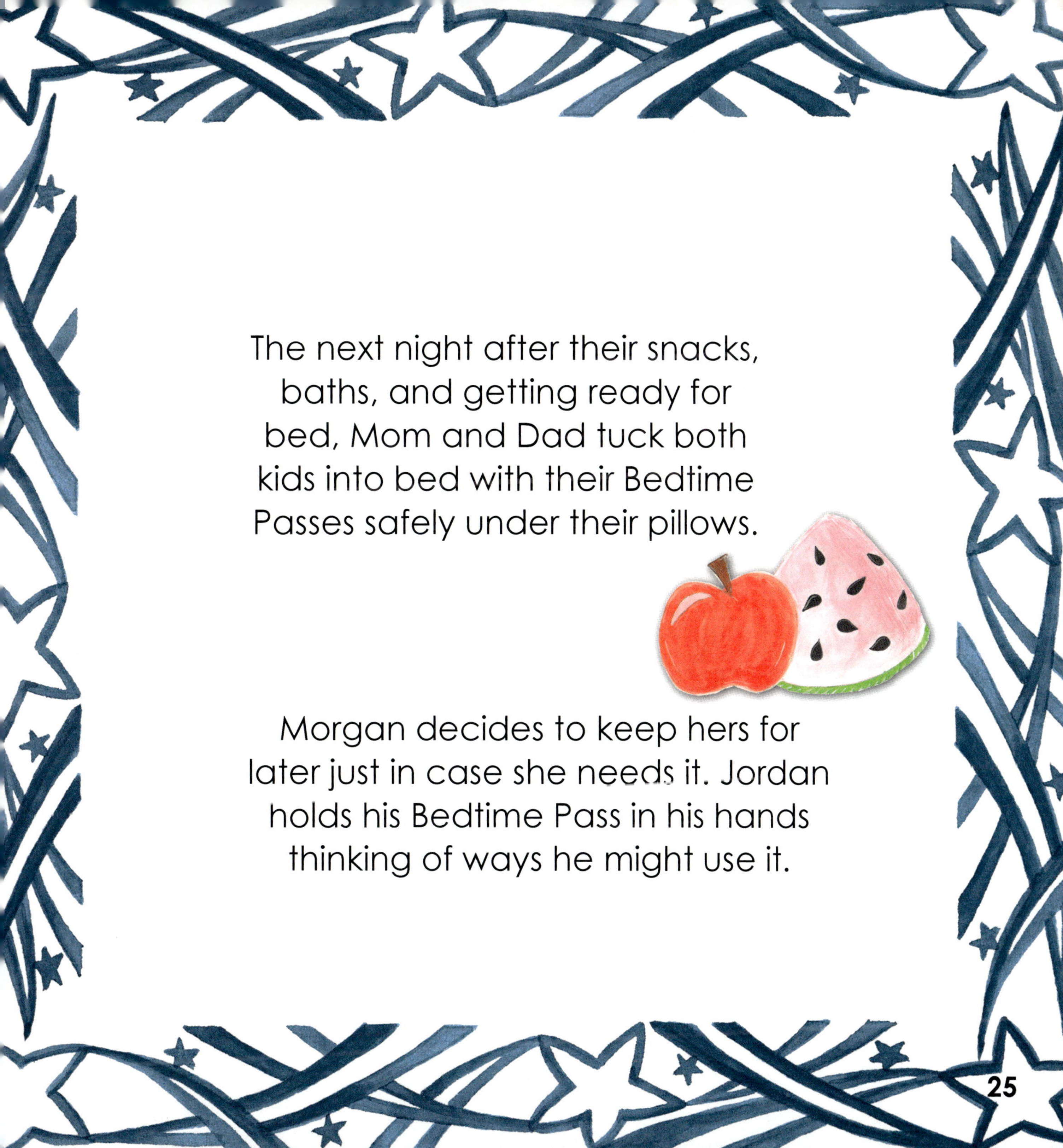

The next night after their snacks, baths, and getting ready for bed, Mom and Dad tuck both kids into bed with their Bedtime Passes safely under their pillows.

Morgan decides to keep hers for later just in case she needs it. Jordan holds his Bedtime Pass in his hands thinking of ways he might use it.

J
M

What happens next?

No playing?

No laughing?

No crying?

No climbing in and out of bed for one more drink?

No more stories?

No more hugs?

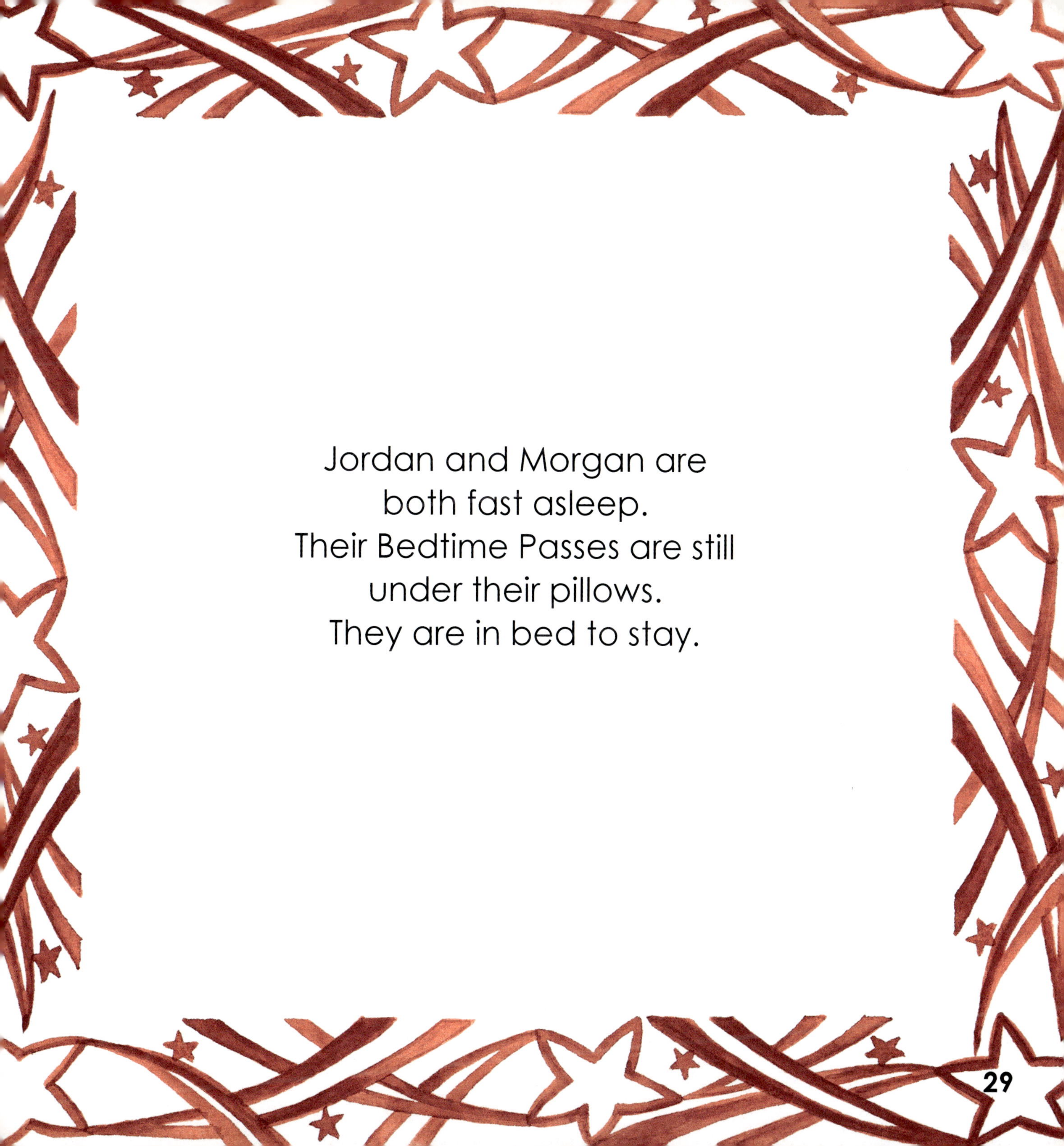

Jordan and Morgan are
both fast asleep.
Their Bedtime Passes are still
under their pillows.
They are in bed to stay.

Goodnight, sleep tight.

Made in the USA
Columbia, SC
12 June 2019

Made in the USA
Las Vegas, NV
01 October 2025